THE BEST OF
carole king
BEGINNING PIANO SOLO

Cover photo: KMazur/WireImage/Getty Images

ISBN 978-1-4803-3873-9

HAL•LEONARD®
CORPORATION

7777 W. BLUEMOUND RD. P.O. BOX 13819 MILWAUKEE, WI 53213

In Australia Contact:
Hal Leonard Australia Pty. Ltd.
4 Lentara Court
Cheltenham, Victoria, 3192 Australia
Email: ausadmin@halleonard.com.au

Visit Hal Leonard Online at
www.halleonard.com

contents

I FEEL THE EARTH MOVE

Words and Music by
CAROLE KING

Moderate Rock

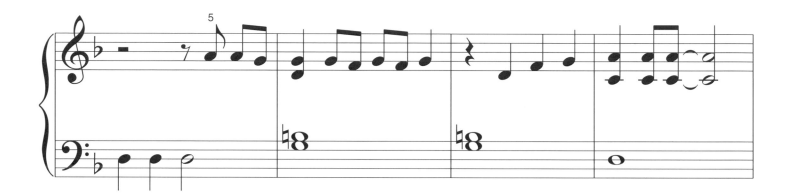

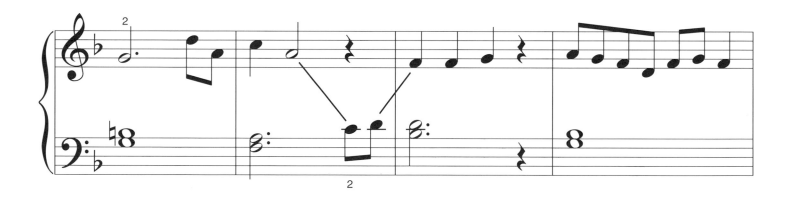

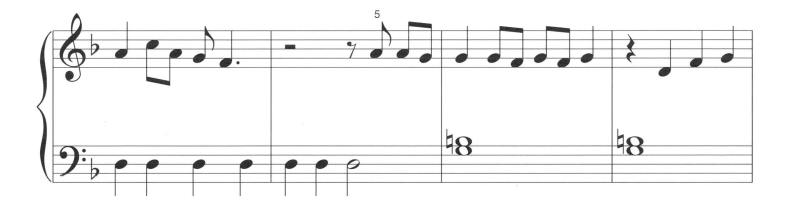

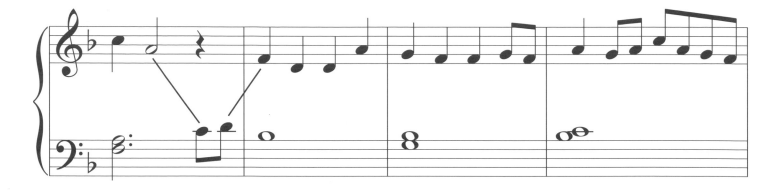

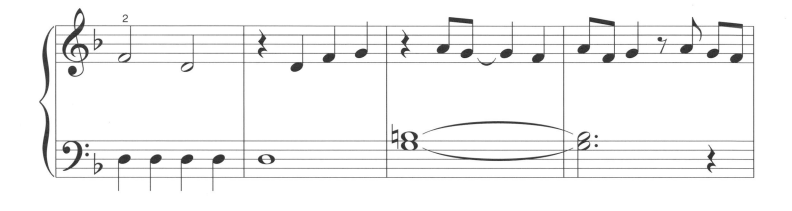

HOME AGAIN

Words and Music by
CAROLE KING

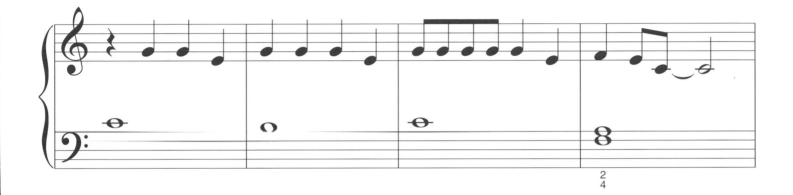

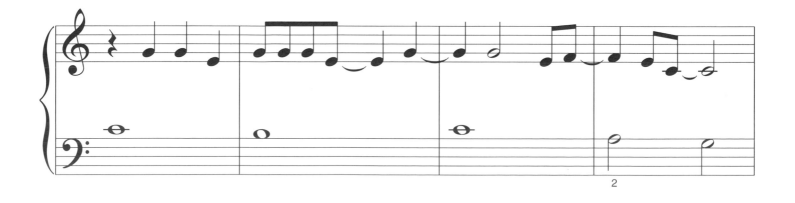

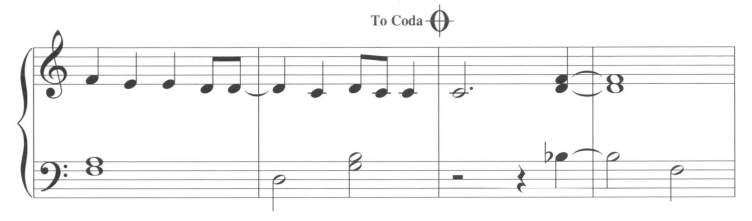

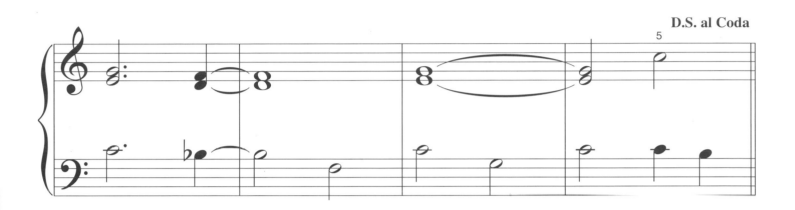

IT'S TOO LATE

Words and Music by CAROLE KING
and TONI STERN

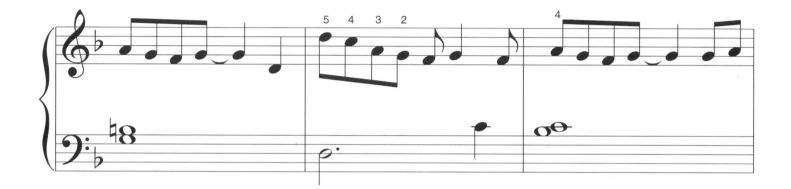

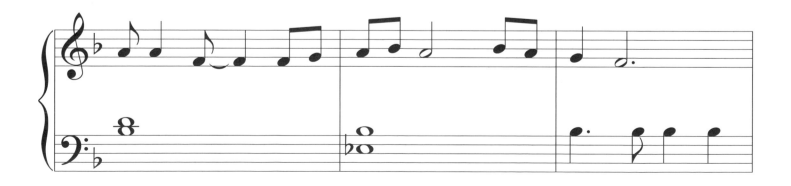

(You Make Me Feel Like)
A NATURAL WOMAN

Words and Music by GERRY GOFFIN,
CAROLE KING and JERRY WEXLER

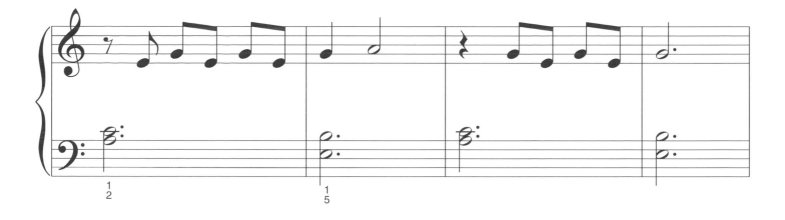

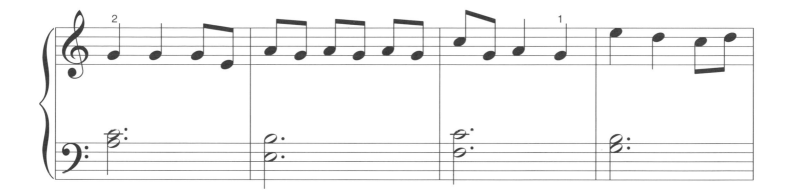

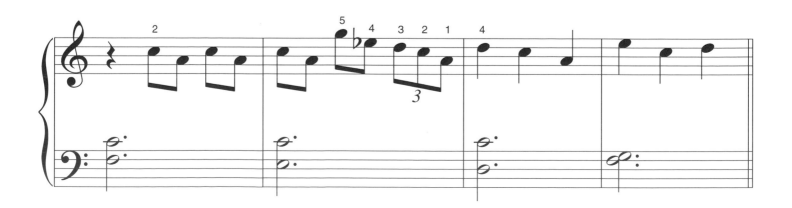

SO FAR AWAY

Words and Music by
CAROLE KING

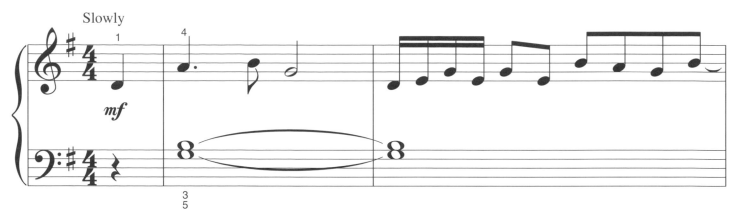

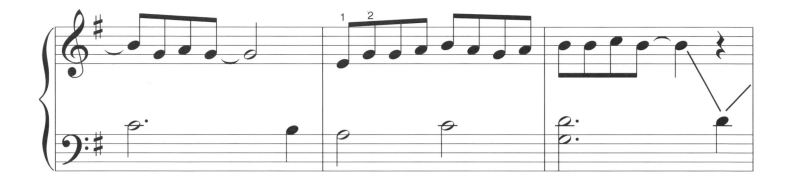

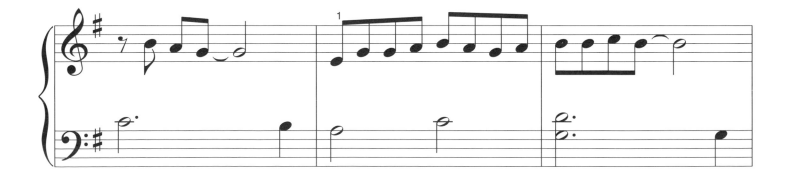

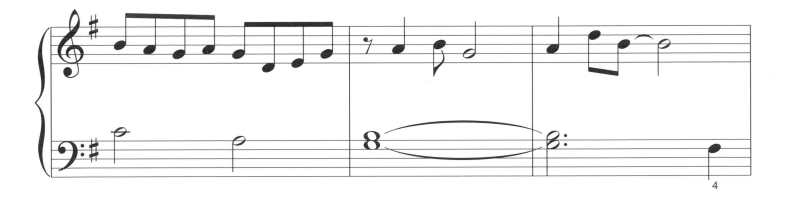

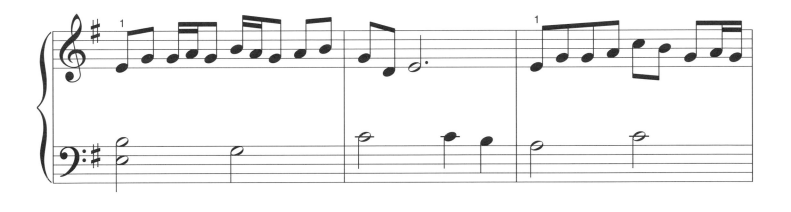

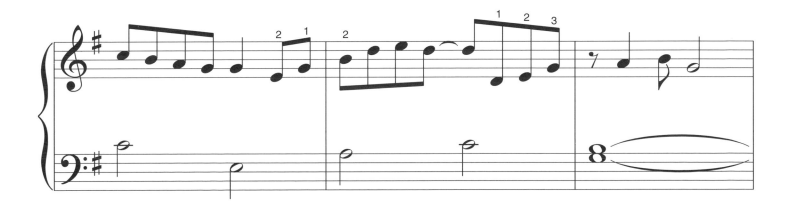

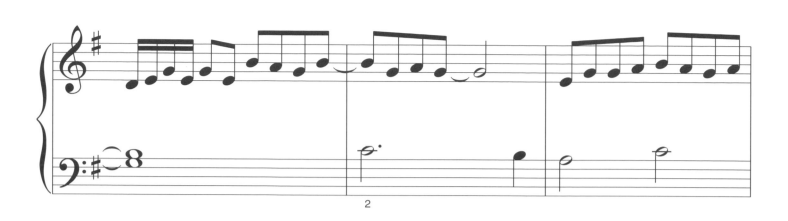

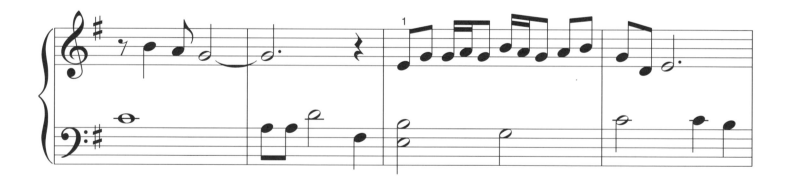

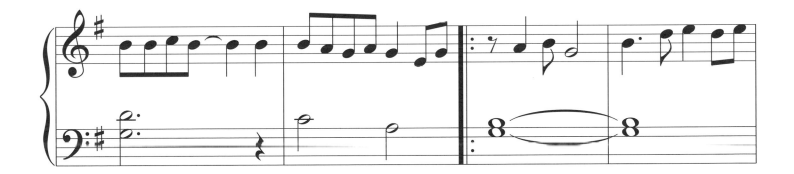

UP ON THE ROOF

Words and Music by GERRY GOFFIN
and CAROLE KING

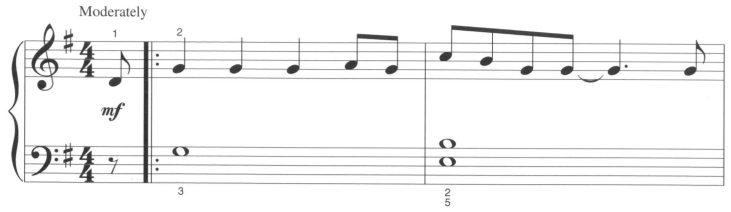

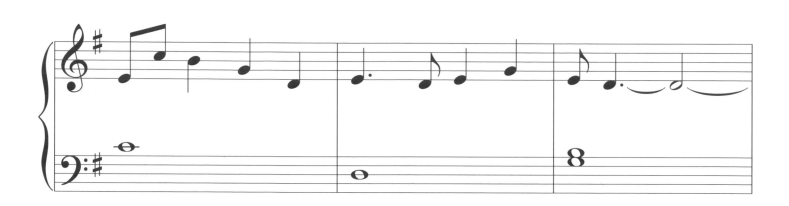

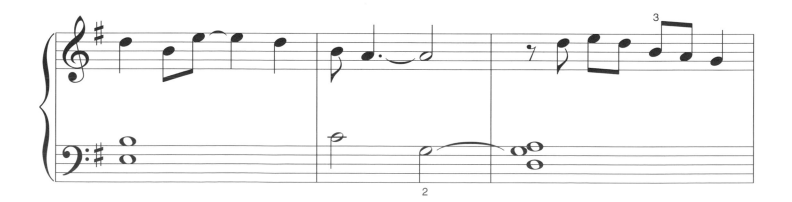

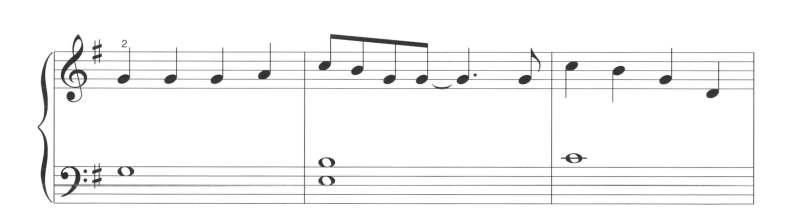

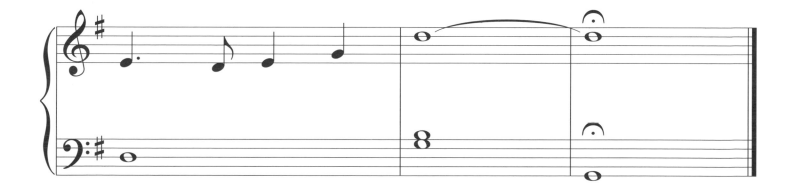

WILL YOU LOVE ME TOMORROW

Words and Music by GERRY GOFFIN
and CAROLE KING

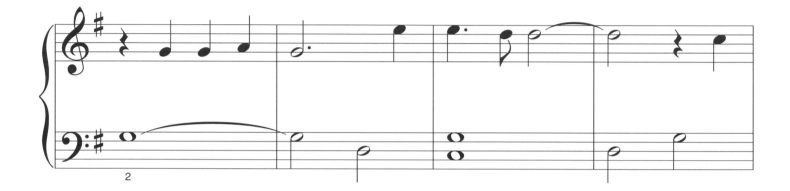

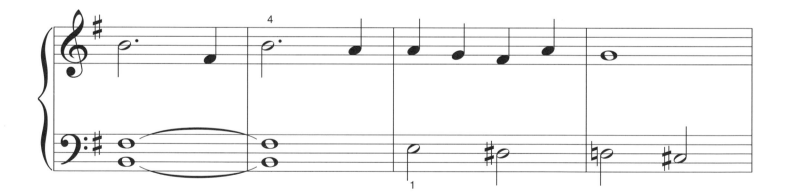

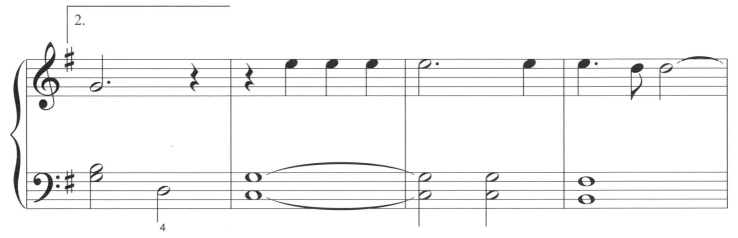

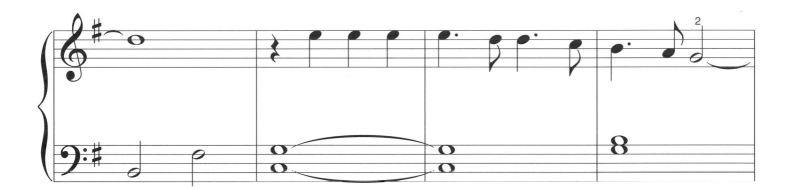

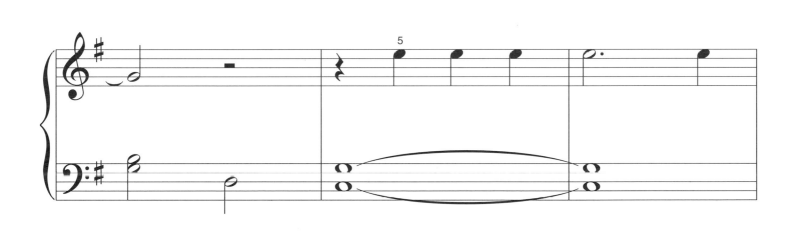

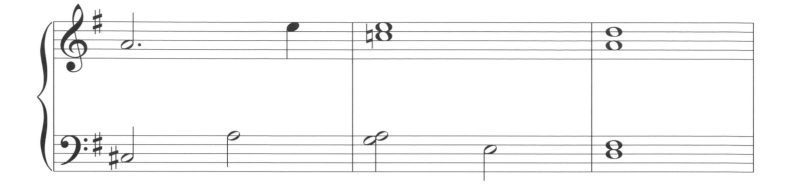

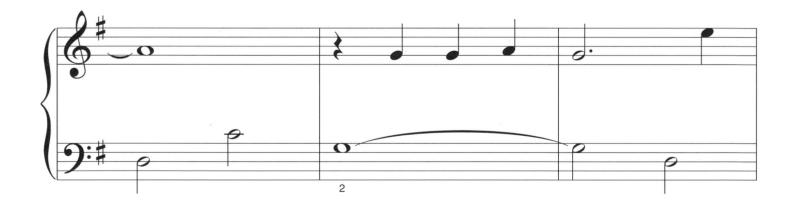

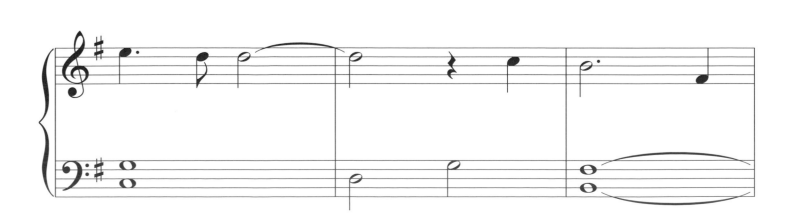

YOU'VE GOT A FRIEND

Words and Music by
CAROLE KING

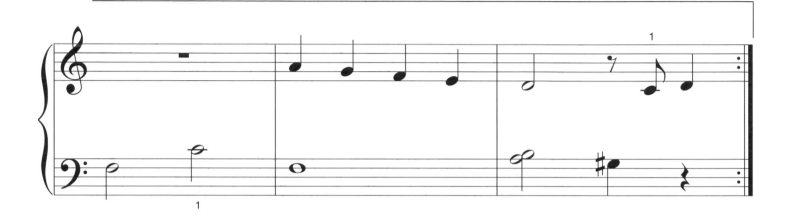

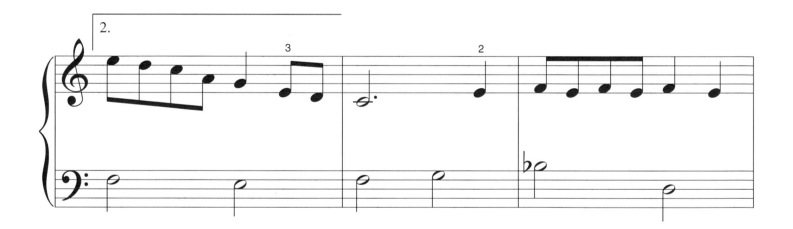

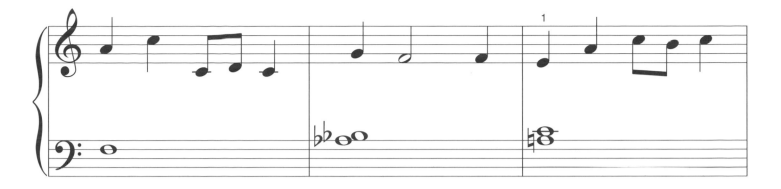

D.S. al Coda

CODA